5 6 7 8

5 6 7 8
Recent Work Press
Canberra, Australia

Copyright © the Authors, 2016

National Library of Australia
Cataloguing-in-Publication entry.
5 6 7 8/ Monica Carroll, Jen Crawford, Owen Bullock, Shane Strange
ISBN:9780994456533 (paperback)
Subjects: Australian poetry

A821.

All rights reserved. This book is copyright. Except for private study, research, criticism or reviews as permitted under the Copyright Act, no part of this book may be reproduced, stored in a retrieval system, or transmitted in any form by any means without prior written permission. Enquiries should be addressed to the publisher.

Cover design: Recent Work Press
Set in Baskerville by Recent Work Press

recentworkpress.com

5 6 7 8

Monica Carroll Jen Crawford

Owen Bullock Shane Strange

RECENT
WORK
PRESS

Contents

5

The sweetest gear	9
Average	10
The five everyday things	11
Driving	12
A surgeon	13
I give you five matches	14
Throttle Switch B Circuit Malfunction	15
Monster	16
The famous	17
Each question is worth five marks %	18

6

frost hollows	25
there is that in which the chaff is put	26
hex	28
circulation i	29
circulation ii	30
circulation iii	32
a hover, a honey	33
cella	36
cul	37
call	38

7

fragments	41
imagine pattern	42
7x7	45
cycles of 7	46
virtues	48
49	50
sleepless	51
seven houses, a chapel and a phone box	53
1974	56
No. 7	57

8

Sleep	61
Quantum	62
16hz	63
Ohms	64
Subatomic	65
A Marxist at Ikea	66
Octopus	67
Sentence	68
August is	69
Karl Marx attends to a butterfly	71
Notes and Acknowledgements	72
Biographies	73

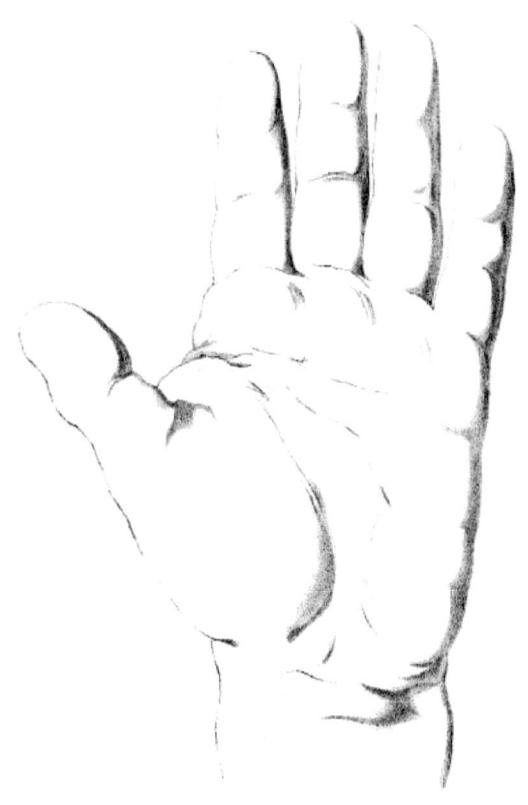

Monica Carroll

The sweetest gear

Hitting it means you're on the cruise. Everything's open. Naked in a good way, like all the windows are down and your hair is loved-up by a warm-fuelled wind. It's not the climax gear but the after, where colour floods back and sweet is the crisp pine tint off the swinging air-freshener.

Average

On average, you get five years. Half a decade after the moment they tell you. But, that's on average. Nine four and two averages out to five. No one actually gets five. I spent a lot of time in the corridor looking down at the gymnasium that was never used. Its shadows seemed less dusty, less deep from above. Sometimes, there'd be badminton. Sometimes small tennis (tabled). For these, the lights warmed. If you write a story about someone losing their thumb, the thumb can be Rosencrantz, later on. Never be afraid to show the depth of your ignorance. Not knowing is not shameful. We not know almost everything.

The five everyday things

Kicking a footy. Catching a ferry. Waiting for the casino to be built. Taking a tunnel. Shoving a handbag.

Wishing for silence to be final.

Driving

in the two-door five-seater, the 2x4 across your lap.
You didn't want to bash the old man for money he'll
never have. We lit cigs from the hot spiral to be cool.
Frags of your durry stick to the heat as you puff puff
to get her going. You jam the lighter in the hole, giving
the car a drag. In back, Knighty and Poof scrape baby
food from glass jars with a metal spoon they share.
The noise shits me. "Quick about it," I tell you as
I brake at the flats. Poof throws a jar at the bricks.
You're walking back already. No wood; just an old
man with a blood-run face tagging. "Better give him a
lift to Calvary," you say, "Squeeze the fuck over, Poof."

A surgeon

A surgeon opens your body without permission or plan.

A surgeon opens your body and sees the fragments of your mother.

A surgeon opens your body to climb inside and hide from the Registrar.

A surgeon opens your body giving black to the x-ray monks of white.

A surgeon opens your body noting a delay in the tee-off time.

A surgeon opens your body celebrating May Day by splashing a bit of claret around the room.

A surgeon opens your body laying traps for the mice that nibble at your heart edges.

A surgeon opens your body misplacing her salami sub and serviette.

A surgeon opens your body whistling at the mass of tumour squeezing your colon.

A surgeon opens your body after pashing the nurse in pre-op, re-tasting the cherry of her lip-gloss.

A surgeon opens your body never having read your poems.

I give you five matches

Make them into thirteen, I say.

Without breaking any, you do.

Throttle Switch B Circuit Malfunction

The first time was speed across a gullied dirt road. The tin can Torana bounced beyond my steering and landed chin first in a ditch.

Next was something in the Cortina. We were in Ballarat. That's all I remember.

A rear-end in the Falcon. Peak hour. No damage.

A rear-end in the Falcon. Turn Left At Any Time With Care: we both pushed off; she braked for air. I late-braked for her. She had a Doctor's appointment booked before she planned the accident.

The last is for next Friday. I've had my eye on the big Scribbly at the left bend of Chuculba Avenue.

Monster

Seats fill in patterns until the show-ground becomes We and emptiness is overtaken by the buzz of waiting. There will be no rain.

The tanker damps the dust as children run relay between the bleachers. Underneath the clown's rainbow curly wig is a white round helmet. The tray of The Bear Claw tipples its last load of five dollar passengers. Little arms waving above the growl of the beast's heart. Between the breezes of cigarette smoke comes the spice of dagwood dog. Large bellied men and faithful following women file along the gully, preferring to watch and walk rather than pay the extra fee for a chair. Marker flags flank the dirt ramps, each leading to a grave of metal bodies, windowless, lightless, gutted and broken as a teen after tequila Tuesday. The stallions ride out on their wide rimmed steads. Gorgeous in ego. A noise bleeds from your ears and everything quakes. Alive inside you the circuits of flowers. The rain won't come. Edging us all with the premise of cool but leaving us dry and full.

The famous

I is third prime number; a regular polygon

An only and odd untouchable, atomic marker of boron

Points on a starfish, Romans hail me V

I stands for dwarfs and all plain senses

The Tradesmen in Chaucer guild me

Fingers & toes, the wounds of Jesus, Pillars of Islam

Rings of Olympus, Beethoven's best

Give it to me high:

I am the rule for food dropped

Give it to me basic:

water earth air fire ether

Each question is worth five marks %

Question 1

1. Marlowe stuck a brooch in his eye.

2.

3. The lion had a dagger jammed in his paw.

4. Sebastian fainted at the claws in his heart, put there by an angel.

5. In the voodoo doll of Capote we stab the arrows mostly around hands, feet and groin like they taught us at karate school.

Question 2

1. Turing hid under floorboards.

2. Anne Frank is hidden behind words.

3. You hide your light under a teapot and your shekels in your socks.

4.

5. I hide everything in stories; lies, dreams, recipes, and the Shroud of Turin, which is actually just the cinnamon in Persian shortbread.

Question 3

1. It takes four lines and four corners to make a square and a rectangle – the difference is equality.

2. The problem with feminism is that it's run by women.

3.

4. You know that feeling, where you ate too much dinner so someone makes the joke from Monty Python and you think, yeah, but he exploded his guts all over the tablecloth – is that really what you want?

5. That feeling of the ordinary surface where all the pain is hidden down deep, pushing aside your body for its own piercing shaft but overhead, the water stays pacific.

Insert number

☐ We all have human rights even though some of us are not very good people.

☐ It's not enough to win by a point or two; annihilation is the aim.

☐ Most volleyball injuries are from spiking.

Answer Key

pg 14

pp 18-21   *Question 1*   5

Question 2   5

Question 3   5

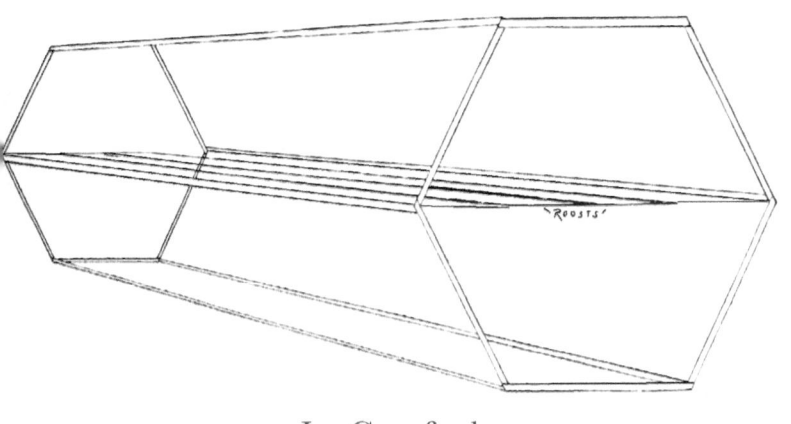

Jen Crawford

frost hollows

cold air drains slowly in the evenings

                                        when it is clear and still

        onto the lowest ground

                          and remains immobile there

there is that in which the chaff is put

you when you walk across the soft dirt are in the wheel tracks.
the shipping was riddled before you found out. now droplets
fall from each container, exerting no force on your path.

the stairs at this point are still wooden, spokes,
your awning the wind. I could be wishing you free use
when you want scaffolding in iron to the blue above,

ten storeys of stairs in crate-wood in care of an ague.
I wouldn't do that. behind us sunlight reflects iron palings.
time to empty the plastic bag. nine am before

the green glass glimmers a plane. this needs temperature
consistently above ground, or it needs defence
which is why no one will defend it. without sunnies

your eyes hurt. stacked vents shine in the earth,
unpainted so you look with no circumference.
now do I walk past a spaceship renovation

taking the call that he's a body? what do the dead
want of us. what do the dying make of their new scene.
nearly home. they are coming out our ears

and the sky not empty but tensile. the coffin a pie-crust.
the sky's soft basket wicked of its snakes.

hex

a soft coughing from the journalist pallbearers. with the screwdriver the man makes the sign of the screw, and all kinds of spaces open up. when you wear a bright vest you're allowed. you just touch it with that and nothing will be the same again. he performs a demonstration, in which she falls back without will the same into his arms. this is a monstrum, a wonder. on the one hand in which it's cut into six pieces, which doesn't happen in the dream: the arm whirring like a blade and screaming in its rotator cuff. outside the hall the pieces need to be smaller. on the other he says I don't expect to physically feel it, but they shiver as they pass into me. the demonstration is into six pieces, which means that the back is separated from the torso. we become the violence that is given, which is not something he or I personally make. at the centre of this is the formation of a word, a sacred threshold. he cannot yet say 'shoe' but makes the sign of the screw with his fingers. no surface of slate with impenetrable grates will ever be the same again. this is a public demonstration of feeling. for care the feeling is taken in six pieces. the sixth is the piece of the back, which answers the questions: what does your body mean? are you passive about your body?

circulation i

dale and his girlfriend nina come back to mum's house with me
to see this place they haven't been. sort of late

teen tourists in a span of life. poppa's dying
his luminous death in mum and jim's bed.

dale and nina stack up horizontally in the bed
beside him, their heads forming a short column of two

like they're conjoined at the neck. their watching him quietly
is a service to my family and that's the night.

at the same time they're keeping the luminosity.
then dale's alone, and mum watches while he sleeps.

circulation ii

it falls over the edge and we go to chase it falls over the edge
we go to chase I have paste for that kind of rift I have six
friends who would like to host the water falling over the edge
in their garden that is a trampoline quivering out

it is a beginning that each one wants the ball but after his
molars are pushing up through we find another child hands
us the ball that is another lamp leading back and forth to the
edges where soreness tips

she asks you what it is the four of them in motion their hair
so long we haven't bought scissors for the water in their faces
tipping away like a ball if we're sore in a little circle around a
credit card account we find a way to chase

into the corner at the glass shelf while he covers his face we
walk in circles through the howling that is a zebra and that
is a giraffe against the world that makes noises suitable for its
names he is refusing because they're too sweet

giving me a tiny edge of fine hairs on the fine edge of his
mother comes only for a day we touch the cut to their warm
garden made of green water with lilies take the swelling for
she comes for a day leaves on sun

when you are more tired you crawl and when you are more
tired you sit as the ball rolls to an atom skirting on a fine rim
we go and take some words with us that he's learned to clap to
see the water shake over the edge

circulation iii

sweetheart they have to be even if you don't remember sweetheart they have to be even if you don't remember sweetheart they have to be even if you don't remember sweetheart they have to be sweetheart they have to be sweetheart they have to be even they have to be even they have to be even they have to be even if you don't remember even to be even if you don't remember even to be even if you don't remember where they have to be you don't remember where they have to be you don't remember where they have you don't remember where they have you don't remember where they have you don't remember where they have to be you have to be you don't remember where you have to be they have to be you don't remember where they have to be they have to be you don't remember where you have to don't remember you have to don't remember you have to don't remember to don't remember to don't remember to don't remember even if to be they have to be you even if to be they have to be you even if to be they have to be somewhere even if to be they have to be somewhere even if somewhere even if somewhere they have to be somewhere even if somewhere they have to be somewhere they have to be where they are to be somewhere they have to be where they are to be somewhere they have to be where they are to be somewhere where they are somewhere where they are somewhere where they are they are somewhere where they are they are somewhere where they are they are somewhere

a hover, a honey

>cell. early 12c.,
>"small monastery, subordinate monastery"
>(from Medieval Latin in this sense),

>later "small room for a monk
>or a nun in a monastic establishment;
>a hermit's dwelling" (c.1300),

>from Latin *cella*
>"small room, store room, hut,"

>related to Latin *celare*
>"to hide, conceal."

The Latin word represents
PIE root **kel-* "conceal"
(source also of Sanskrit *cala* "hut, house, hall;"

Greek *kalia* "hut, nest,"
kalyptein "to cover,"
koleon "sheath,"
kelyphos "shell, husk;"

    Latin *clam* "secret;"
        Old Irish *cuile* "cellar,"
        celim "hide,"
            Middle Irish *cul* "defense, shelter;"

        Gothic *hulistr* "covering,"
            Old English *heolstor*
            "lurking-hole, cave, covering,"
                Gothic *huljan* "cover over,"
                hulundi "hole," *hilms* "helmet,"
            halja "hell,"

           Old English *hol* "cave,"
           holu "husk, pod").
        Sense of monastic rooms
        extended to prison rooms (1722).

Used in 14c., figuratively,
of brain "compartments;"
used in biology by 17c.
of various cavities
(e.g. wood structure,
segments of fruit, bee combs),

gradually focusing to the modern sense
of "basic structure of living organisms"
(which OED dates to 1845).

Electric battery sense is from 1828,
based on original form
Meaning "small group of people
working within a larger organization"
is from 1925

Cell body is from 1851;
cell division from 1846;
cell membrane from 1837
(but *cellular membrane* is 1732);
cell wall from 1842.

cella

under the air conditioning vent
a little bell is ringing softly.
I hope that you are sleeping.

the union poster lifts.
I hope to return your book to you soon.
a little bell is ringing softly.

we sleep lightly while you feed
then return as adults to the world.
squares of sunlight press their angles open.

the doors hiss open, then close.
the little bell is ringing softly.
I hear no footsteps through the glass.

cul

high wind in the valley of silver birches.
your mother and your father shout at each other, with laryngitis.
they are shouting for each other.

the birches throw their shadows to one side.
on the bright pavilion she takes forty calls.
these are the animals needing rescue today.

call

liquid tree above the roof. leaves in water.
leaves blink on and off. branches hold their place.
cloud bank holds its place, a form reaching back, stillness
being the one you want to return to. little hands
and a misplaced kiss. cloud expanding upon you,
holding its form. summer put your backpack on.
check the sky then leave the house. from antill st
you see the mountain blinking. call home, hear him rustle
the phone to his ear. listen, breathe, look up.

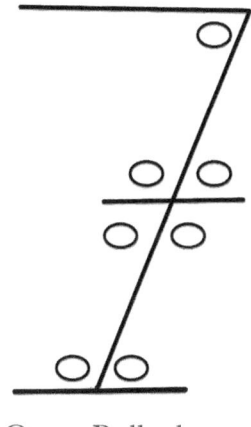

Owen Bullock

fragments

seven neck
vertebrae

seven fans
in the structure of a guitar

the perfect number
in belief

seven days
(based on seven planets)
now twenty-four-ed

summer is heaven
in 77
Marc Bolan sang
in the year he crashed

Star Wars came out (I was ten)
I went to see *A Star Is Born*
pretending to be 14

the original numeral
all about angles

imagine pattern

no one imagines how much time it takes
writing a letter in blood
coaxing life out of *columns*
going backwards from *Mill's Mess*
unwinding *Burke's Barrage*

those who've gone before
                trap and free

                throw me a word
I'll give a pattern

no one imagines how much time
writing a letter in blood
learnt between hemispheres
      by the time I reached the end
half my possessions were things to throw
      I juggled
because I couldn't multi-task –
      our world demands it

    those who've gone before

        trap and free

no one imagines

writing a letter in blood

and between hemispheres

by the time I reached the end

I could juggle six balls

but not drive a car

the car must be driven

  to get to the running event

    to get to the juggling festival

      to get to work

like writing a letter in blood

I grasped a few catches

of s e v e n balls

instead of earning money

raising children

vying for office

by the time I reached the end
I had achieved nothing
      and my everything
what I could carry

between hemispheres
how to learn
repeated in music
and research –
I never imagined how easy it could be
to succeed

I finally failed properly
going backwards
from *Mill's Mess*
the machine, the Frauberg shuffle
the giraffe, the penguin
shower, reverse
see-saw, double-see-saw
and tricks I invented myself
      the play things of a child . . .
no one understands how difficult they are

7x7

after Stead

the angel of regret sli-
ding down the bannister to
an empty hall like a bombed
outhouse and you watching from
across the road, exposure
painted more pitiful than
any play as fundraiser

cycles of 7

no memories

only a vague

lost feeling

14

it begins

thinking for myself

first child

and an old rusty key

on a cake

that's just maturity

she tells me

hearing the shift

35 – I return

to the spawning grounds

with my three children

42

solitude is the lesson

before love

reaching

the high plateau

I walk on

virtues

coming home
sitting in silence
until
we give our reflections
think again					peacefulness

carrying
the hot water
the breakfast
it's what you carry
the potter told me				compassion

mending the spare tent
solving the shed
releasing plants
each problem
finds rest between us				collaboration

to the higher self
obedient –
a word which
could cramp the loins
spear the heart   obedience

reading each other
sharing friends
the day of rain
sunny as the heat
as the privacy of moonlight   friendship

they keep moving
like stones in the river
some discarded
some poems
in the estuary   creativity

these bodies aging
I must also look to
care for myself . . .
rains fall
on the reading tent   acceptance

49

49 today . . . by this time
my heroes were dead
Baxter (42), Plath (30)
van Gogh (37), Hendrix (27)
I've achieved greater
happiness than I thought possible
the poems, paintings, songs
drift away
with rain that surrounds the tent
with the river
that commands leaves and stones
to rush to the sea
emptying itself out
overnight, so that the raging
rumbling of stones, wind's
lash, come to nothing and
the river's dropped, we say
in the morning

sleepless

meditation stutters

but the river

keeps on

still haven't reached the island

socks

and blankets

dark night

don't have to be happy

to sleep

milk farmer's motorbike

about

5 a.m.

denying sleep

the haiku

that escape

the river dictates

but I don't have a pen

or the language

snores

rock the bed

mine

seven houses, a chapel and a phone box

the nearest neighbours arguing
i would watch them from my den below our hedge
in the no-man's-land between property and clay pit
the kids that came there
played with me
and haunted my free days

the nosey and dozey couple below them
had a house of mod cons
which we vilified
because we couldn't envy
they made elderflower champagne
watched the royal wedding in colour
later, a bookish man bought the house
and wrote me a ticket for another world
where his alternative friends hung on the walls like clever bats

we often had to cross the yard
of the house with the dog

to get to the woods

and the reliable well

their house smelled of rice pudding

though they never made it

the father often away

the mother a kind welcome in her shriek

the true old Cornish couple

kept the hamlet and the next house alive

their high teas a pantry opened out

after a broad embrace at the top of their winding

beflowered path –

their son kept a horse called Lion in the lane

opposite the people whose name only we knew

who had visitors day in day out

but never us

the rag & bone man from over the downs

almost as dirty as the coalman

a crooked smile from his truck

a part for an engine or fence

a huge spider hung over their marvellous bath

and us, toilet outside, no hot water

a well that froze in winter

dried up in summer

the men had always worked in the mine

and I feared it

water ran down the walls

but not the frozen windows

toes stretched towards the bone-cold bed end

there was silence

or there was shouting

everyone had their meals separate

and strayed

over the hills

1974

What is it I'm searching for – Slade, *Far Far Away* – something I never had? I didn't go to parties, only watched (only seven). Those anthems and costumes . . . a link to *My Oh My* – I'd given up on pop music by then. This version also lip-synched, for the Roy Hudd show (2008). As the credits roll, the announcer says in an unbelievably plummy accent, 'The final programme in this series from the Palace Theatre in Manchester can be seen at the same time next week'.

No. 7

the little girl points out
a castle
on Black Mountain

old guy –
resisting the urge
to untangle his braces

over and over
she says
the bus is wobbly like a jelly

mirror
the driver's tongue
going round the corner

she insists

up close

people need space

man writing

his bullet

points

her vibrant smile

leaps onto the bus

with her

Shane Strange

Sleep

upbraids the mind through the dull hours:
       through the knife cuts of fluorescent lighting;
the photocopier's eight-fold ways
       —teasing like a pool of honey.

But in the small hours
       waking chases sleep away, leaving
the footfalls of roof possums,
       the Doppler effect of passing drunks and,
from other nights in other towns,
       the echo of trains, and
the memory of the echo of trains.

Quantum

Observations have revealed that I be and be not.
Schrödinger's Hamlet. Apparent when noticed,
otherwise assumed to confirm the Standard Model.
Additionally, outrageous fortune is no longer available
in arrow form, but appears as a thousand hairline slits
up the skin of your arms, like a phase experiment, or
an attempt to map some reptilian forebear.

Ophelia, when
does love act as a particle,
and when as a wave?

Look
how infinite
I am.

16hz

They speak a mellifluous language of their own, pitched somewhere between a wheel of cheese and velveteen. I know. I've swelled a scene or two, felt the vibrations through the refreshment table, or in the corners where I mumble. I've learned beauty strikes them between certain frequencies: a mundane sonance. I can identify the euphony, but not always its cause. I must have missed the memo, or had it misread to me. Untuned, I submerge beneath sonar range, below human hearing: evolving in dark waters, like weird fishes; or an octabass, 1850, Jean Baptiste Vuillame, 16hz.

Ohms

We stood in the old powerhouse while the musicians stood in the old powerhouse we stood in the old powerhouse while the musicians stood in the old powerhouse we stood in the old powerhouse while the musicians tuned up tuned up tuned up tuned up we stood in the old powerhouse while the musicians tuned up against the old powerhouse stood while the musicians tuned up against we stood in the old powerhouse while the musicians tuned up against the machine. fossil. record.

For a single movement Reich's *Eight Lines* transmitting up concrete and for a single movement there was no child, no labour, no obligation that could stop us lifting our eyes in a single movement our eyes in a single movement lifting our eyes in a single movement into the sun our eyes into the sun contrapuntal.

Subatomic

The Mayor of Hiroshima marks each nuclear test
with a letter of condemnation for the relevant
head of state. Copies are posted on walls in
the Peace Memorial Museum near:
the watches arrested (at the second of impact);
the (burnt-to-coal) contents of school lunch boxes;
the National Railway ticket (dated August 6, 1945).
In the clean light of the Australian
War Memorial, I am arrested
by a gas mask for a dog
(World War I this time)
its form hollow for the head within:
the most tiny quantity
of reality.
Remember to breathe, I think.
But remember at the molecular level
even oxygen has
atomic weight.

A Marxist at Ikea

Children, yelling and jabbing each other with three inch pencils, jumped out at them as they walked the labyrinth through laminate wardrobes and integral hinges. He kept saying 'What is this? What do we do here?' and she didn't know. Her head was filled with A-rings and diareses, though she knew in Swedish they did not apply. He ran a finger across the in-store map, hoping for a sign. She brewed a headache born of the sounds of 6 billion people vying for coffee tables, and white fabric standard lamps. The fight they had, she told me later, was about an '8 or, maybe, a 10', which was seismic by their standards. They had to sit in the car for 20 minutes while the shuddering passed.

Then I told her of some friends of mine who had travelled across Europe eating only at Ikea cafeterias. Why? she asked. Because, I said, no one noticed if you paid.

Octopus

tease me into every ink with fine
impossible behaviours.

I tolerate leather, and he
skin—bilateral symmetry.

deimatic octopode, a choice
to make: saddle stitching;

impossible glove? I am
the beast below the surface.

Sentence

1. You told me time moved forward: each moment a brick upon the last.

2. I am old enough now to suspect the truth of such things.

3. Tramping two tight circles in the grass, we mimic birds on thermal winds.

4. I am surprised to meet you in this fruitless display.

5. Your wings are bare, and you break each eye you meet against the roof of your mouth.

6. This time, don't believe me when I tell you to fly.

7. You know how the story ends: the ashes sifted from dry mouths; the papers piled high, left drying in corners.

8. Why did I think this time would be different?

August is

I.

never the harvest

or the end of the footy season.

my son's birthday (isn't)

for building and for bringing down

the earth's tilt

sun redux

Sextilis.

II.

Αύγουστος:

my grandmother desperate

to find the words

for *άνθος δελφίνι*

(delphinium)

a petal for each month

before dying.

V.

a rocky beach in Italy

where all was closed

I longed for you to leave

so I could finish drawing

the vineyard and

we crawled along the coast

in buses that threatened

to stumble off cliffs

and into the sea

as Caesar did.

Karl Marx attends to a butterfly

In London, gravity kept *Herr Doktor Professor* firmly on a chair as if a singularity had bought him there and not his pen. Until it was home to the wife and kids again. In later years, on Hampstead Heath, like any good bourgeois, he would sit and stare across the morning sun. His worries about money gone. And Engels kept in Manchester running mills, no longer reminded of the gravity, of situations & c. Sick children. Money for the rent. Weights around his neck.

Delighting in his grandchild, a butterfly falls across his hand. And Karl Marx lifts it on a breeze to watch its wings multiply against the sun from two to four to eight. A trick of the light. Or, possibly, just the way he sees. Value, he remembers, is immaterial but nonetheless real.

Notes and Acknowledgements

'frost hollows' from L.D. Pryor, *Trees in Canberra*. Canberra: Dept of the Interior, 1962

'a hover, a honey' from etymonline.com

'7x7' previously appeared in *Takahe* and 'imagine pattern' in the chapbook *tracer* (Ampersand Duck, 2015).

'16hz' previously appeared in *foam:e* (foame.org)

Biographies

Monica Carroll is a writer, poet and post-graduate student at the University of Canberra. Her creative work has been widely awarded and anthologised within Australia and abroad. Her research interests include phenomenology, touch, poetics and space.

Jen Crawford's poetry publications include *Admissions* (Five Islands Press, 2000), *Bad Appendix* (Titus Books, 2008) , *Pop Riveter* (Pania Press, 2011) and *Koel* (Cordite Books, 2016). She is an Assistant Professor of Creative Writing at the University of Canberra.

Owen Bullock publications include *urban haiku* (Recent Work Press, 2015), *breakfast with epiphanies* (Oceanbooks, NZ, 2012) and *sometimes the sky isn't big enough* (Steele Roberts, NZ, 2010). He won the Canberra Critics' Circle Award for Poetry 2015. He is a PhD Candidate in Creative Writing at the University of Canberra.

Shane Strange lives in Canberra. His writing has appeared in various print and on line journals, including *Overland, Griffith Review, Burley, Verity La, foam:e* and *Cordite Poetry Review*. He is currently studying at the University of Canberra, where he also tutors and lectures in Creative Writing.

More Recent Work

Owen Bullock	*Urban Haiku (2015)* *River's Edge (2016)*
Paul Hetherington	*Gallery of Antique Art (2016)*
Niloofar Fanaiyan	*Transit (2016)*
Prose Poetry Project	*Pulse (2016)*
Jen Webb	*Sentences from the Archive (2016)*
Monica Carroll, Jen Crawford, Owen Bullock & Shane Strange	*5 6 7 8 (2016)*
Subhash Jaireth	*Incantations (2016)*
Shane Strange	*Notes to the Reader (2015)*

all titles available from
recentworkpress.com

www.ingramcontent.com/pod-product-compliance
Lightning Source LLC
Chambersburg PA
CBHW020624300426
44113CB00007B/771